Published By Nicholas Thompson

@ Parker Mulcahy

Cooking With Sirtfoods: Managing Blood Sugar Naturally

and Love Your Heart, Love Your Food

All Right RESERVED

ISBN 978-87-94477-19-2

TABLE OF CONTENTS

Breakfast Scramble

Ingredients:

- A handful of thinly sliced mushrooms

- Take 0.17 ounce parsley, finely chopped

- Add a seed mixture for topping and some Rooster Sauce for flavor 0.70 ounce kale, roughly chopped

- 0.166 ounce extra virgin olive oil

- 0.166 ounce mild curry powder

- ½ bird's eye chili, thinly sliced

- 2 eggs

- 0.166 ounce ground turmeric

Directions:

1. Mix the curry and turmeric powder, then apply a little water until a soft paste has been produced.

2. Steam up the kale for 2–3 minutes.

3. Use medium heat to warm oil in a frying pan and fry the chili and mushrooms for 2–3 minutes before they start browning and softening.

4. Add the eggs and spice paste, and cook over medium heat, then add the kale and continue cooking for another minute over medium heat.

5. Attach the parsley, then blend well and enjoy.

Summer Berry Smoothie

Ingredients:

- 0.5 ounce honey optional

- 14 ounce apple juice can also use almond milk, skim milk, coconut milk or another flavor of the Juice

- One banana sliced

- 14 ounce frozen mixed berries

- 6 ounce vanilla Greek yogurt

- Optional garnish: fresh berries and mint sprigs

Directions:

1. In a blender, put the apple juice, banana, berries, and yogurt; blend until smooth.

2. If you think the texture of the smoothie is too thick, add the liquid (1/4 cup) a bit more.

3. Taste and, if desired, add the honey. Do a topping of fresh berries and mint sprigs if needed, then squeeze into two cups.

Miso And Sesame In Ginger And Chili Stir-Fried Greens

Ingredients:

- 1 Tablelitre Mirin

- 2 garlic nails

- 1 teaspoon of fresh ginger, finely chopped

- Cup 3/4 (50 g) kale, cut

- 2 sesame seed teaspoons

- Buckwheat: 1/4 cup (35 g)

- 1 teaspoon of turmeric powder

- 2 extra virgin olive oil teaspoons

- Miso paste: 31/2 teaspoons (20 g)

- 1 x 5-ounce (150 g) firm tofu block

- 1 celery stalk (40 g), trimmed (about 1/3 cup
  when sliced)

- 1/4 cup (40 g) red, sliced onion

- 1 medium (120 g) zucchini (when cut, around
  1 cup)

- 1 chile thai

- 1 teaspoon tamari (or soy sauce, unless gluten
  is avoided)

Directions:

1. Oven gas to 400oF (200oC). Line a small,
   parchment-paper roasting pan.
2. Mix both the mirin and the miso. Lengthwise
   cut the tofu, then diagonally split each slice
   into triangles in half.

3. Cover the tofu with the miso mix and leave to marinate as the other Ingredients: are packed.

4. Slice the angle into the celery, red onion, and zucchini. Chop the chili, garlic and ginger thinly, then set aside.

5. Cook the Kale for 5 minutes in a steamer. Discard and set aside.

6. Place the tofu in the roasting pan, sprinkle the tofu with the sesame seeds and roast in the oven for 15 to 20 minutes until it has been nicely caramelised.

7. Wash the buckwheat in a sieve, then place it along with the turmeric in a saucepan of boiling water. Cook as directed by package, then drain.

8. Heat the oil in a frying pan; add the celery, onion, zucchini, chili, garlic and ginger and fry over high heat for 1 to 2 minutes, then reduce to medium heat for 3 to 4 minutes until the

vegetables are cooked through, but are still crunchy.

9. If the vegetables start sticking to the pan you may need to add a tablespoon of water.

10. Add the tamari and kale, and cook for another minute.

11. Serve with the greens and buckwheat, when the tofu is ready.

Turkey Escalope With Sage, Capers, And Parsley And Spiced Cauliflower

Ingredients:

- 2 Tablespoons of turmeric soil

- 1/2 cup (30 g) of sun-dried, finely chopped tomatoes

- 1/4 cup (10 g) fresh, chopped parsley

- 1/3 pound (150 g) steak or turkey cutlet (see above)

- Dried sage Teaspoon

- 1/4 Lemon Juice

- Cauliflower: 11/2 cups (150 g), finely chopped

- 2 Cloves of garlic, finely chopped

- 1/4 cup (40 g) red, finely chopped onion

- 1 Thai chili, finely chopped

- 1 Teaspoon of fresh ginger, finely chopped

- 2 Spoonfuls of extra virgin olive oil

- 1 Tablelit capers

Directions:

1. Place the raw cauliflower in a food processor to make the "couscous" Pulse to finely chop the cauliflower in 2-second bursts until it resembles a couscous. Alternatively, you should use a razor, then finely cut it.

2. In 1 tablespoon of the butter, fry the garlic, red onion, chili and ginger until soft but not browned.

3. Attach the cauliflower and turmeric, and simmer for 1 minute. Remove from heat and

add the tomatoes that have been sun-dried, and half the parsley.

4. Coat the turkey escalope in the sage and a little oil, then fry in a frying pan over medium heat for 5 to 6 minutes using remaining oil, turning regularly.

5. Add the lemon juice, remaining parsley, capers and 1 table spoon of water to the pan when cooked through. That will make a cauliflower sauce to serve.

Chicken Diet

Ingredients:

- 50g buckwheat

- For the salsa

- 130g tomato (about 1)

- 1 bird's eye chilli, finely chopped

- 1 tbsp capers, finely chopped

- 5g parsley, finely chopped

- Juice of ¼ lemon

- 120g skinless, boneless chicken breast

- 2 tsp ground turmeric

- juice of ¼ lemon

- 1 tbsp extra virgin olive oil

- 50g kale, chopped

- 20g red onion, sliced

- 1 tsp chopped fresh ginger

Directions:

1. To make the salsa, remove the eye from the tomato and chop it very finely, taking care to keep as much of the liquid as possible. Mix with the chilli, capers, parsley and lemon juice. You could put everything in a blender but the end result is a little different.

2. Heat the oven to 220ºC/gas 7. Marinate the chicken breast in 1 teaspoon of the turmeric, the lemon juice and a little oil. Leave for 5–10 minutes.

3. Heat an ovenproof frying pan until hot, then add the marinated chicken and cook for a

minute or so on each side, until pale golden, then transfer to the oven (place on a baking tray if your pan isn't ovenproof) for 8–10 minutes or until cooked through.

4. Remove from the oven, cover with foil and leave to rest for 5 minutes before serving.

5. Meanwhile, cook the kale in a steamer for 5 minutes. Fry the red onions and the ginger in a little oil, until soft but not coloured, then add the cooked kale and fry for another minute.

6. Cook the buckwheat according to the packet instructions with the remaining teaspoon of turmeric. Serve alongside the chicken, vegetables and salsa.

Sirtfood Bites

Ingredients:

- 1 tbsp ground turmeric

- 1 tbsp extra virgin olive oil

- the scraped seeds of 1 vanilla pod or 1 tsp vanilla extract

- 1–2 tbsp water

- 120g walnuts

- 30g dark chocolate (85 per cent cocoa solids), broken into pieces; or cocoa nibs

- 250g Medjool dates, pitted

- 1 tbsp cocoa powder

Directions:

1. Place the walnuts and chocolate in a food processor and process until you have a fine powder.
2. Add all the other Ingredients: except the water and blend until the mixture forms a ball.
3. You may or may not have to add the water depending on the consistency of the mixture – you don't want it to be too sticky
4. Using your hands, form the mixture into bite-sized balls and refrigerate in an airtight container for at least 1 hour before eating them. You could roll some of the balls in some more cocoa or desiccated coconut to achieve a different finish if you like.
5. They will keep for up to 1 week in your fridge.

Rocket And Celery Smoothie

Ingredients:

- 1 stalk of rosemary

- 1 shot of water

- 100g parsley

- 50g lettuce

- 20g rocket

- 1 cucumber

- 2 limes

- 1 celery stalk

Directions:

1. First, the rocket, parsley and lettuce have to be cleaned and plucked a little smaller.

2. Then the cucumber has to be peeled and possibly cut into smaller pieces. We press a juice from the lime and we only need the needles from the rosemary.

3. All Ingredients: are put into the blender, liquefied with a little water and mixed thoroughly.

4. The smoothie can now be enjoyed. A little tip: A celery leaf can be used as a decoration.

Golden Turmeric Latte

Ingredients:

- 1 teaspoon raw honey

- Pinch of black pepper

- Small piece of peeled ginger

- Pinch of cayenne pepper

- 3 cups of coconut milk

- 1 teaspoon turmeric powder

- 1 teaspoon cinnamon powder

Directions:

1. The preparation is very easy, we just put all the Ingredients: in a blender and mix

everything well. After that, everything is

heated in a pan for a few minutes.

Olive Oil-Braised Pole Beans

Ingredients:

- 2 fresh flat-leaf parsley sprigs

- 1 fresh rosemary sprig

- 1 dried bay leaf

- 1 pound pole beans, trimmed

- 2 cups vegetable stock

- Freshly squeezed juice of ½ lemon

- 1 medium yellow onion, thinly sliced

- ½ medium fennel bulb, thinly sliced

- 4 garlic cloves, thinly sliced

- Peel of 1 lemon

- ¾ cup   extra virgin olive oil

- Kosher salt and freshly ground black pepper

- 2 fresh thyme sprigs

Directions:

1. In a medium stockpot, combine the onion, fennel, garlic, lemon peel, oil, and ¼ cup water. Season with salt and pepper, cover and simmer over medium heat, stirring occasionally, until the vegetables are translucent, about 15 minutes.
2. Tie the thyme sprigs, parsley sprigs, and rosemary sprig together with butcher's twine to make a bouquet garni.
3. Add the bouquet garni and the bay leaf to the vegetables. Add the pole beans, stock, and lemon juice and stir to combine.
4. Season with salt and pepper. Bring the mixture to a simmer, and cover, and cook, stirring occasionally, until the pole beans are very tender, about 1 hour 30 minutes.
5. Remove and discard the bay leaf and bouquet garni. Season with salt and pepper.

6. Using a pair of tongs, transfer the pole beans and vegetables to four plates or to one large serving plate.

Feta Sage Muffins

Ingredients:

- 3/4 cup low-fat milk

- 3/4 cup low-fat plain yogurt

- 1/3 cup plus 2 tablespoons of extra virgin olive oil

- 1/3 cup chopped fresh sage

- 2 garlic cloves, minced

- 1 1/4 cup whole wheat pastry flour

- 1/2 cup finely ground yellow cornmeal

- 2 tablespoon coconut palm sugar or other granulated sugar of choice

- 1 teaspoon baking powder

- 1/2 teaspoon baking soda

- 1/4 teaspoon salt

- 1 cup canned (drained and rinsed) or cooked dried chickpeas

- 1 cup diced feta cheese

Directions:

1. Preheat oven to 350 degrees F. In a large bowl, mix together the flour, cornmeal, sugar, baking powder, baking soda and salt.

2. In a blender or food processor, whirl together chickpeas, milk, yogurt, olive oil, sage and garlic until smooth.

3. Pour chickpea mixture into dry INGREDIENTS:and mix gently. Fold in feta. Divide batter among 12 standard-sized greased or paper lined muffin cups.

4. Bake for 20 minutes, or until a toothpick inserted into the center of a muffin comes out clean.

5. Let cool several minutes before unfolding. Best served warmed.

Kale With Scrambled Eggs

Ingredients:

- 3 huge eggs, softly beaten

- At least of fit salt

- At least of ground pepper

- 2 cut entire grain bread, toasted

- 2 teaspoon canola oil

- 1 ½ cups kale (1/2 ounces)

- ½ cup new raspberries

Directions:

1. Warmth oil In at least nonstick skillet over medium-high warmth. Include kale and cook until shriveled, frequently blending 1 to 2 minutes.

2. Move the spinach to a plate. Wipe the skillet clean, place over medium warmth, and include eggs.

3. Cook, mixing a couple of times to ensure in any event, cooking until simply set, 1 to 2 minutes.

4. Mix In the spinach, salt, and pepper. Serve the scramble with toast and raspberries.

Avocado And Kale Omelet

Ingredients:

- 2 tablespoon lime juice

- 2 tablespoon cleaved new cilantro

- 2 teaspoon unsalted sunflower seeds

- Spot of squashed red pepper

- Spot of salt

- 3 enormous eggs

- 2 teaspoon low-fat milk

- Spot of salt

- 3 teaspoons extra-virgin olive oil, partitioned

- 1 cup cleaved kale

- ¼ avocado, cut

Directions:

1. Mix eggs with milk and salt In at least a bowl. Warmth 1 teaspoon oil In at least nonstick skillet over medium warmth. Include the egg blend and cook until the bottom is about, and therefore the inside remains somewhat runny 1 to 2 minutes.

2. Flip the omelette over and cook until set, around 30 seconds more. Move to a plate.

3. Hurl kale with the staying one teaspoon oil, juice, cilantro, sunflower seeds, squashed red pepper, and slightly of salt. Top the omelette with the kale plate of mixed greens and avocado.

Vegetable Salad

Ingredients:

- 1 chopped chicory head

- Chopped parsley, 10 g

- Arugula, 1 tbsp

- Roughly chopped celery leaves,

- Extra virgin olive oil, 1 tbsp

- Lemon juice, ½ tbsp

- Mustard, 1 tsp

- 1 finely chopped apple

- Chopped celery, 200 g

- One roughly chopped red onion

- Roughly chopped walnuts, ½ cup

Directions:

1. Mix the celery, arugula, onion, walnuts, and parsley in a bowl and toss together.

2. Mix the extra virgin olive oil, lemon juice, and mustard. Drizzle over the salad and enjoy!

Quinoa And Avocado Salad

Ingredients:

- 1 small pink grapefruit, peeled and finely cut

- 1 handful arugula

- 1 cup baby spinach leaves

- 2 tbsp extra virgin olive oil

- 2 tbsp lemon juice

- 1 cup quinoa

- 2 cups water

- 1 large avocado, pitted and sliced

- ¼ radicchio, finely sliced

- Salt and black pepper, to taste

Directions:

1. Wash quinoa in a fine sieve under running water for 3-4 minutes, or until water runs clear. Set aside to drain, then boil it in two cups of water for 16 minutes.

2. Fluff with a fork and set aside to cool. Stir avocado, radicchio, arugula and baby spinach into cooled quinoa.

3. Add grapefruit, lemon juice, and olive oil, season with salt and black pepper and stir to combine well.

Strawberry Buckwheat Pancakes

Ingredients:

- 250 milliliters milk

- 2 teaspoons olive oil

- Freshly squeezed juice of 1 orange

- 100 grams strawberries, chopped

- 100 grams buckwheat flour

- 1 egg

Directions:

1. Pour the milk into a bowl and mix in the egg and a teaspoon of olive oil.

2. Stir the flour into the liquid mixture until smooth and creamy.

3. Allow it to rest for 15 minutes.

4. Heat a little oil in a pan and pour in a quarter of the mixture (or to the size you prefer).

5. Sprinkle in a quarter of the strawberries into the batter.

6. Cook for around 2 minutes on each side.

7. Serve hot with a drizzle of orange juice.

Sirtfood Mueslo

Ingredients:

- 1 /8 cup (15 grams) walnuts, chopped

- 1(1 /2) tablespoon (10 grams) cocoa nibs

- 2 /3 cup (100 grams) strawberries, hulled and chopped

- 3 /8 cup (100 grams) plain Greek yogurt (or vegan alternative, such as soy or coconut yogurt)

- 1 /4 cup (20 grams) buckwheat flakes

- 2 /3 cup (10 grams) buckwheat puffs

- 3 tablespoons (15 grams) coconut flakes or dried coconut

- 1 /4 cup (40 grams) Medjool dates, pitted and chopped

Directions:

1. Mix all the Ingredients: (leave out the strawberries and yogurt if not serving right away).

Creamy Strawberry & Cherry Smoothie

Ingredients:

- 1 tablespoon plain full-fat yogurt

- 6fl ounces unsweetened soya milk

- 3½ ounces strawberries

- 3 ounces frozen pitted cherries

Directions:

1. Place the Ingredients: into a blender then process until smooth. Serve and enjoy.

Strawberry & Citrus Blend

Ingredients:

- ½ avocado, peeled and de-stoned

- ½ teaspoon matcha powder

- Juice of 1 lime

- 3 ounces strawberries

- 1 apple, cored

- 1 orange, peeled

Directions:

1. Place Ingredients: into a blender with enough water to cover them and process until smooth.

Rocket And Arugula

Ingredients:

- 1.4 ounce rocket leaves

- 1 ounce red wine

- Salt as required

- 8 ounce arugula

- 2.8 ounce pear

- 0.35 ounce toasted walnuts

- 0.35 ounce yogurt (curd)

- Powdered black pepper as required

- 0.43 ounce virgin olive oil

- 1 ounce of lemon juice

- 1 ounce balsamic vinegar

Directions:

1. Wash the pears, remove and break them into thin pieces under running water.
2. Soak them up and cool them in a medium bowl filled with red wine.
3. Whisk balsamic vinegar, pure olive oil, and lemon juice together in a bowl to make the dressing for the salad.
4. With this dressing, toss the rocket and arugula in a medium bowl and sprinkle salt and black pepper powder over the leaves.
5. Put the poached pears nicely around the salad and top with yogurt and toasted walnuts.

Chocolate Berry Smoothie

Ingredients:

- Add 250 ml (8 ounce) milk of your choice

- One very ripe banana

- 0.5 ounce maple syrup

- 0.5 ounce chia seeds

- 0.33 ounce cocoa powder or cacao

- Add 3.52 ounce (3/4 cup) mixed frozen berries (I use a mix of blackberries, raspberries, blackcurrants, and redcurrants)

Directions:

1. Place in a blender and scramble all the Ingredients: until smooth. Pour into a glass, then serve.

Smoked Salmon Omelet

Ingredients:

- 0.083 ounce Capers

- 10 g Rocket, chopped

- 0.166 ounce Parsley, chopped

- 2 Medium eggs

- 3.52 ounce Smoked salmon, sliced

- 0.166 ounce Extra virgin olive oil

Directions:

1. Crack eggs into a bowl. Add the tuna, capers, parsley, and shot.

2. In a non-stick frying pan, fire up the olive oil until heated but not smoking.

3. Add the egg mixture and move the mixture around the pan, using a spatula or fish slice until it is even.

4. Reduce heat, and let it cook through the omelet.

5. Insert the spatula around the edges and roll the omelet up or fold in half to serve.

Kale And Red Dal Onion With Bukkwheat

Ingredients:

- 1 thai chili, finely chopped

- 1 teaspoon of mild curry powder (mean or warm, if you prefer)

- 2 tablespoons of turmeric soil

- 11/4 cups of vegetable stock (300ml) or water

- 1/4 cup (40 g) dried, rinsed lentils

- Cup 3/4 (50 g) kale, cut

- 31/2 pounds (50ml) of tinned coconut milk

- 1 cup of extra virgin olive oil

- 1 pound of mustard seeds

- 1/4 cup (40 g) red, finely chopped onion

- 2 cloves of garlic, finely chopped

- 1 teaspoon of fresh ginger, finely chopped

- Buckwheat: 1/3 cup (50 g)

Directions:

1. Heat the oil over medium heat in a medium saucepan, and add the mustard seeds. When the mustard seeds begin popping, add the onion, garlic , ginger and chili. Cook until tender, for about 10 minutes.

2. Connect the turmeric curry powder and 1 tablespoon, then simmer the spices for a few minutes. Stir in the stock and bring to a boil.

3. Add the lentils to the saucepan and simmer for another 25 to 30 minutes until the lentils are cooked through and a smooth dal is present.

4. Add milk to the kale and coconut and simmer for another 5 minutes.

5. In the meantime, cook the buckwheat with the remaining turmeric tablespoon, as per the box instructions. Drain alongside the dal, and serve.

Aromatic Chicken Breast With Kale And Red Onions And A Chili Salsa Tomato

Ingredients:

- 1 teaspoon of fresh chopped ginger

- Buckwheat: 1/3 cup (50 g)

- To the salsa

- 1 medium sized tomato (130 g)

- 1 thai chili, finely chopped

- 1 mezzanine capers, finely chopped

- 2 table cubits (5 g) of parsley, finely chopped

- 1/4 pound (120 g) of skinless, boneless breast chicken

- 2 tablespoons of turmeric soil

- 1/4 lemon juice

- 1 litre, extra virgin olive oil

- Cup 3/4 (50 g) kale, cut

- 1/8 cup (20 g) raw, sliced onion

- 1/4 lemon juice

Directions:

1. Remove the eye from the tomato to make the salsa, then slice it very good, making care to preserve as much of the liquid as possible. Mix with the chili, capers, lemon juice and parsley.

2. You could bring it all in a blender but the end product is a little different.

3. Heat the oven to 220 ° C (425oF). In 1 teaspoon of turmeric, the lemon juice, and a

little oil, marinate the chicken breast. Leave on for five to ten minutes.

4. Heat an oven-proof frying pan until hot, then add the marinated chicken and cook on each side for about a minute or so until pale golden, then move to the oven (set on a baking tray if your pan is not oven-proof) for 8 to 10 minutes or until cooked.

5. Remove from the oven, cover with foil, then leave for 5 minutes to rest before serving.

6. Meanwhile, boil the kale for 5 minutes in a steamer.

7. Fry the red onions and the ginger in a little oil, then add the cooked kale and fry for another minute until soft but not browned.

8. Cook the buckwheat with the remaining turmeric teaspoon, as per package instructions. Serve with chicken, vegetables, and salsa.

Harissa Baked Tofu With Cauliflower "Couscous"

Ingredients:

- 1/4 Lemon Juice

- Firm tofu 7 ounces (200 g)

- Cauliflower: 13/4 cups (200 g), roughly chopped

- 1/4 cup (40 g) red, finely chopped onion

- 1 Teaspoon of fresh ginger, finely chopped

- 2 Tablespoons of turmeric soil

- 1/2 cup (30 g) of sun-dried, finely chopped tomatoes

- Red bell pepper: 3/8 cup (60 g)

- 1 Half Thai Chili

- 2 Garlic Nails

- About 1 cubiccup extra virgin olive oil

- Pinch of cumin to the ground

- Pinch of coriander

- 1/2 cup (20 g) minced parsley

Directions:

1. Oven gas to 400∘F (200∘C).

2. Slice the red pepper lengthwise around the core to make the harissa so you have nice flat slices, remove any seeds, then place the chili and one of the garlic cloves in a roasting pan.

3. Add a little oil and the dried cumin and coriander and roast for 15 to 20 minutes in the oven until the peppers are soft but not too brown. (Leave the oven on at this setting.) Cold, then mix with the lemon juice into a food processor until smooth.

4. Lengthwise slice the tofu and then diagonally cut into triangles each half. Place in a small non-stick roasting pan or one lined with parchment paper, cover with harissa and roast for 20 minutes in the oven — the tofu should have absorbed the marinade and turned dark red.

5. Place the raw cauliflower in a food processor to make the "couscous" Pulse to finely chop the cauliflower in 2-second bursts until it resembles a couscous. Alternatively, you should use a razor, then finely cut it.

6. Thin out the remaining clove of garlic. In 1 teaspoon of oil, fry the garlic, red onion and ginger, until soft but not browned, then add the turmeric and cauliflower and cook for 1 minute.

7. Remove from heat and stir in the tomatoes and parsley, which are dried with sun. Serve with the tofu which is fried.

Strawberry Buckwheat Tabouleh

Ingredients:

- 20g red onion

- 25g medjool dates, pitted

- 1 tbsp capers

- 30g parsley

- 100g strawberries, hulled

- 1 tbsp extra virgin olive oil

- Juce of ½ lemon

- 50g buckwheat

- 1 tbsp ground turmeric

- 80g avocado

- 65g tomato

- 30g rocket

Directions:

1. Cook the buckwheat with the turmeric according to the packet instructions. Drain and keep to one side to cool.

2. Finely chop the avocado, tomato, red onion, dates, capers and parsley and mix with the cool buckwheat.

3. Slice the strawberries and gently mix into the salad with the oil and lemon juice. Serve on a bed of rocket.

Breakfast With Omelette

Ingredients:

- 2 walnuts

- 1 portion of the parsley-arugula mix

- 1 slice of buckwheat bread

- 1 teaspoon of olive oil

- 2 eggs

- 1 cup of baby spinach

Directions:

1. Start by preheating your pan. While it is preheating, break 2 eggs in a bowl, add the spinach to it and whisk. Add this egg mixture to the pan and voila!

2. To continue preparation, place the green mix, walnuts and bread on the side on a large

plate. Here is your sirtfood diet breakfast ready

Green Juice

Ingredients:

- 3 to three stalks of celery, including the leaves

- ½ green apple

- juice of half a lemon

- ½ teaspoon matcha powder

- 3 big hands of kale

- A large handful of arugula

- A very small hand of flat leaf parsley

- A very small hand of lovage leaves

Directions:

1. First, squeeze the kale, rocket, parsley and

    lovage in the juicer (approx. 50ml).

2. Then juice the apple and celery and squeeze

    the lemon. Now mix everything and divide

    into two glasses.

3. Dissolve the matcha powder in one

    half. When everything is well dissolved, add

    the rest of the juice and enjoy.

Smoothie Based On Goggins And Mats

Ingredients:

- 20g dark chocolate (at least 85% cocoa content)

- 1 date

- ½ teaspoon turmeric

- 1 to 2 mm from a Thai chili, finely chopped

- 200ml unsweetened almond milk

- 100g unsweetened Greek yogurt

- 6 half walnuts

- 8-10 medium-sized strawberries

- A handful of kale leaves

Directions:

1. Simply put everything in a blender and mix well.

2. Enjoy

Sirtfood Green Juice

Ingredients:

- 2 to 3 large celery stalks (5 1⁄2 ounces or 150g), including leaves

- 1/2 medium green apple

- 1/2- to 1-inch (1 to 2.5 cm) piece of fresh ginger

- Juice of 1/2 lemon

- 2 large handfuls (about 2 1⁄2 ounces or 75g) kale

- A large handful (1 ounce or 30g) arugula

- A very small handful (about 1⁄4 ounce or 5g) flat-leaf parsley

- 1/2 level teaspoon matcha powder

Directions:

1. Mix the greens (kale, arugula, and parsley) together, then juice them. We find that juicers can really differ in their efficiency at juicing leafy vegetables, and you may need to rejuice the remnants before moving on to the other ingredients.

2. The goal is to end up with about 2 fluid ounces or close to 1/4 cup (50ml) of juice from the greens.

3. Now juice the celery, apple, and ginger.

4. You can peel the lemon and put it through the juicer as well, but we find it much easier to simply squeeze the lemon by hand into the juice. By this stage, you should have around 1 cup (250ml) of juice in total, perhaps slightly more.

5. It is only when the juice is made and ready to serve that you add the matcha. Pour a small amount of the juice into a glass, then add the

matcha and stir vigorously with a fork or teaspoon.

6. Once the matcha is dissolved, add the remainder of the juice. Give it a final stir, then your juice is ready to drink. Feel free to top up with plain water, according to taste.

Grilled Garlic Mushroom Kabobs

Ingredients:

- 16 jumbo white mushrooms

- 16 whole cloves garlic, peeled

- 1 large yellow onion, cut into 16 pieces with 2 to 3 layers each

- Fine ground sea salt

- Ground black pepper

- 1 tablespoon chopped fresh basil

- Fresh Garlic Olive Oil

- 1/3 cup   extra virgin olive oil

- 4 cloves garlic, smashed and peeled

- Kabobs

- 16 grape or cherry tomatoes

- 8 wooden skewers, pre-soaked

Directions:

1. Preheat the grill to 375 to 400 degrees F.

2. In a small saucepan, stir together the extra virgin olive oil and 4 garlic cloves.

3. Cook over medium heat for 5 minutes. Remove the pan from the heat and let sit while you make the kabobs.

4. To assemble each kabob, take a wooden skewer and slide on a tomato, a mushroom, a piece of onion and a garlic clove.

5. Follow that with another mushroom, another piece of onion, a garlic clove and another tomato. Repeat for all the kabobs.

6. Place the kabobs on a baking sheet and brush with the 1/3 of the   extra virgin olive oil. Sprinkle with salt and pepper.

7. Place the kabobs on the grill. Grill for 6 minutes. Brush the kabobs with another 1/3 of the oil.

8. Flip and grill for another 3 to 4 minutes, until the vegetables are tender.

9. Remove the kabobs from the grill and place on a serving plate.

10. Brush with the remaining oil and sprinkle with more salt, pepper and the fresh basil before serving.

Classic French Toast

Ingredients:

- 2 teaspoon vanilla concentrate

- 1/2 teaspoons ground cinnamon partitioned

- 8 cuts Brioche bread

- 5 huge eggs

- 1/2 cup entire milk

Directions:

1. On the off chance that's utilizing an electric iron, preheat the frypan to 350 degrees F.
2. Race until considerably consolidated.
3. Plunge all sides of the bread In the egg blend. Note - include the opposite portion of the cinnamon after you've plunged half your bread cuts and blend another time. This may

make sure the entirety of the cuts gets an honest measure of cinnamon.

4. Soften at least margarine on the recent frypan or In a large skillet over medium warmth.

5. Serve the French toast warm with syrup, granulated sugar, and berries, whenever wanted.

6. Note-to keeps the French toast warm, heat the stove to 200 degrees F. Spot a wire rack on a huge preparing sheet, and spot the French toast on the shelf. Keep warm In the grill for as long as a half-hour.

Moroccan Spiced Eggs

Ingredients:

- ½ tsp gentle stew powder

- ½ tsp salt

- 2 × 400g (14oz) can hacked tomatoes

- 1 x 400g (14oz) may use chickpeas in water

- At least a bunch of level leaf parsley (10g (1/3oz)), cleaved

- 1 tsp olive oil

- 2 shallot, stripped and finely hacked

- 2 red (chime) pepper, deseed ed and finely hacked

- 2 garlic clove, stripped and finely hacked

- 2 courgette (zucchini), stripped and finely hacked

- 5 medium eggs at room temperature

Directions:

1. Heat the oil In a pan, include the shallot and red (ringer) pepper, and fry delicately for five minutes.
2. At that time, include the garlic and courgette (zucchini) and cook for another moment or two. Include the tomato puree (glue), flavors, and salt and blend through.
3. Add the cleaved tomatoes and chickpeas (dousing alcohol and all) and increment the heat to medium. With the highest of the dish, stew the sauce for a half-hour – ensure it's delicately rising In and permit it to reduce in volume by around 33%.
4. Remove from the heat and blend In the cleaved parsley.

5. Preheat the grill to 200C/180C fan/350F.

6. When you are prepared to cook the eggs,
    bring the spaghetti sauce up to a fragile stew
    and move to at least broiler confirmation dish.

7. Crack the eggs on the dish and lower them
    delicately into the stew. Spread with thwart
    and prepare In the grill for 10-15 minutes.
    Serve the blend in unique dishes with the eggs
    coasting on the highest.

Carrot, Buckwheat, Tomato And Arugula Salad In A Jar

Ingredients:

- 1/2 cup of destroyed cabbage

- 1 tbsp. olive oil

- 1 tbsp. new lemon juice and place of ocean salt

- 1/2 cup sunflower seeds 1/2 cup carrots

- 1/2 cup of tomatoes

- 1 cup cooked buckwheat blended in with 1 tbsp.

- chia seeds 1 cup arugula

Directions:

1. Put Ingredients: in a specific order: dressing, sunflower seeds, carrots, cabbage, tomatoes, buckwheat, and arugula.

Cucumber Salad With Lime And Coriander

Ingredients:

- 2 tablespoons new coriander

- 2 pieces Lime (juice)

- 1 piece Red onion 2 pieces Cucumber

Directions:

1. Cut the onion into rings and daintily cut the cucumber. Slice the coriander finely.

2. Place the onion rings in a bowl and season with about a large portion of a tablespoon of salt. Focus on it well and afterward fill the bowl with water.

3. Pour off the water and afterward flush the onion rings completely (in a strainer).

4. Set up the cucumber cuts with onion, lime juice, coriander, and olive oil in a salad bowl and mix everything great.

5. Season with somewhat salt.

6. You can keep this dish in the cooler in a

    secured bowl for a couple of days.

Strawberry And Nut Granola

Ingredients:

- 1½ teaspoon ground ginger

- 1½ teaspoon ground cinnamon

- 120 milliliters (4fl ounces) olive oil

- 2 tablespoons honey

- 200 grams (7 ounces) oats

- 250 grams (9 ounces) buckwheat flakes

- 100 grams (3(½) ounces) walnuts, chopped

- 100 grams (3(½) ounces) almonds, chopped

- 100 grams (3(½) ounces) dried strawberries

Directions:

1. Combine the oats, buckwheat flakes, nuts, ginger and cinnamon.

2. In a saucepan, warm the oil and honey.

3. Stir until the honey has melted.

4. Pour the warm oil into the dry Ingredients: and mix well.

5. Spread the mixture out on a large baking tray (or two) and bake in the oven at 150ºC (300ºF) for around 50 minutes until the granola is golden.

6. Allow it to cool.

7. Add in the dried berries.

8. Store in an airtight container until ready to use.

Chilled Strawberry And Walnut Porridge

Ingredients:

- 1 teaspoon chia seeds

- 200 milliliters (7fl ounces) unsweetened soya milk

- 100 milliliters (3(½) ounces) water

- 100 grams (3(½) ounces) strawberries

- 50 grams (2 ounces) rolled oats

- 4 walnut halves, chopped

Directions:

1. Place the strawberries, oats, soya milk and water into a blender, and process until smooth.
2. Stir in the chia seeds and mix well.
3. Chill in the fridge overnight and serve in the morning with a sprinkling of chopped walnuts. It's simple and delicious.

Orange & Celery Crush

Ingredients:

- 1 carrot, peeled

- 3 stalks of celery

- 1 orange, peeled

- ½ teaspoon matcha powder

- Juice of 1 lime

Directions:

1. Place Ingredients: into a blender with enough water to cover them and blitz until smooth.

Tropical Chocolate Delight

Ingredients:

- 1 ounces rocket

- 1 tablespoon 100% cocoa powder or cacao nibs

- 5fl ounces coconut milk

- 1 mango, peeled & de-stoned

- 3 ounces fresh pineapple, chopped

- 2 ounces kale

Directions:

1. Place Ingredients: into a blender and blitz until smooth. You can add a little water if it seems too thick.

Apple Pancakes With Blackcurrant Compote

Ingredients:

- 0.166 ounce baking powder

- Take-Two apples then peel them and cut into small pieces

- 300ml partially skimmed milk

- 2 egg whites

- 0.33 ounce light olive oil

- ounce porridge oats

- 4.40 ounce plain flour

- 1 ounce caster sugar

- Pinch of salt

For the compote:

- 4.23 ounce blackcurrants washed and stalks removed

- 1 ounce caster sugar

- 3 tbsp water

Directions:

1. Make the compote first. Transfer the blackcurrants, water, and sugar in a saucepan. Bring to a cooker and simmer for 10-15 minutes.

2. In a big pot, combine the oats, flour, baking powder, caster sugar, and salt and blend well.

3. Stir in the apple and whisk a little at a time in the milk before you have a smooth mix.

4. Whisk the egg whites then insert into the flour for the pancake. Bring the batter over to a tub.

5. Heat 0.083 ounce of oil over medium-high heat in a non-stick frying pan and add approximately one-quarter of the batter.

6. Cook until light brown, on all hands. Remove for four pancakes and repeat to produce.

7. Eat the pancakes drizzled over with blackcurrant compote.

Muesli Sirt

Ingredients:

- Cup 1/4 (40 g) medjool seeds, diced and pitted

- 1/8 cup (15 g), chopped walnuts

- 11/2 cups (10 g) of cocoa nibs

- Buckwheat flakes: 1/4 cup (20 g)

- Buckwheat puffs: 2/3 cup (10 g)

- 3 tablespoons (15 g) of coconut or dry cocoa flakes

- 2/3 cup (100 g) hulled and chopped strawberries

Directions:

1. Pure Greek yogurt (or vegan substitute, such as soy or coconut yogurt) 3/8 cup (100 g)

2. Mix all the Ingredients: together (leave off the strawberries and cream, if not instantly served).

Salmon Fillet Pan-Fried With Caramelized Endive, Arugula, And Celery Leaf Salad

Ingredients:

- Cherry tomatoes, 2/3 cup (100 g), half cut

- 1/8 cup (20 g) red, thinly sliced onion

- 13/4 ounces arugula (50 g)

- 2 spoonfuls (5 g) of celery leaves

- 1 x 5-ounce (150 g) fillet with skinless salmon

- 2 spoonfuls of brown sugar

- Petersil: 1/4 cup (10 g)

- 1/4 lemon juice

- 1 tablelit capers

- 1 clove of garlic, sliced roughly

- 1 litre, extra virgin olive oil

- 1/4 avocado, stoned, peeled, and diced

- 1 endive arm, roughly 21/2 ounces (70 g), halved in length

Directions:

1. Heat the oven to 220 ° C (425oF).

2. Place the parsley, lemon juice, capers, garlic, and 2 teaspoons of oil in a food processor or mixer for dressing and blend until smooth.

3. For the salad, combine the leaves of avocado, tomato, red onion, arugula, and celery.

4. Heat a frying casserole over high heat. Rub the salmon in a little oil and sear for a minute or two in the hot saucepan to caramelize the fish skin.

5. Transfer to a baking tray and place in the oven for 5 to 6 minutes or until it is cooked; reduce the cooking time by 2 minutes if you like the pink served inside of your fish.

6. Wipe the frying pan out meanwhile and put it back on high fire. Mix the brown sugar with the remaining oil teaspoon and sprinkle it over the endive cut sides.

7. Place the cut-sides of the endive in the hot pan and cook for 2 to 3 minutes until tender and beautifully caramelized. In the dressing, toss the salad and serve with salmon, and endive.

Kale And Red Onion With Buckwheat

Ingredients:

- 3 1/3 kale or spinach

- 1 tablespoon olive oil

- 1 small red onion

- 3 garlic cloves

- 2 teaspoons turmeric

- 1 cup of water

- 1 cup of buckwheat

- 1 deseeded chili

- 1 cup of red lentils

- 2 teaspoons garam masala

- 2 cups of coconut milk

- Ginger

Directions:

1. You can start by bringing the Ingredients: into the form you can use. Chop the onions and set them aside. Crush 3 garlic cloves. Grate the ginger.
2. Finely chop the chili and start preparing the dish by preheating a deep and wide saucepan.
3. Take olive oil in a sufficiently preheated saucepan and heat it.
4. Add the onion, reduce the heat, close the lid of the saucepan and cook for 5 minutes until it softens.
5. Add the crushed garlic, ginger and chili in order and continue cooking. Then immediately add the turmeric.
6. Add garam masala and some water as well. Cook for 1 more minute.

7. Continue cooking by adding red lentils, coconut milk and 1 cup of water.

8. Raise heat. Mix everything in the saucepan. Close the lid, reduce the heat and cook for 20 more minutes. Stir occasionally. Feel free to add a little more water if the ingredients stick together.

9. Then add the kale and mix and close the lid again. Let it cook for another 5 minutes. At that point, the cooking time will vary depending on the vegetable you will add. For example, if you use spinach instead of kale, cook it for a maximum of 3 minutes.

10. Now get another saucepan. A medium-sized one is ideal. Put the buckwheat in it and add plenty of boiling water.

11. Bring the water to a boil again and cook for another 10 minutes. If you like it harder, you can reduce this time.

12. If you like softer, there is no harm in cooking
    more. Strain them after they are cooked as
    you wish. Put them on a plate. Put the kale
    mixture on the other side of the plate and
    serve.

Boiled Egg Salad

Ingredients:

- 1 tablespoon of olive oil

- 5 drops of lemon

- Salt, cumin, paprika to taste

- 1 hard-boiled egg

- 1 small red onion

- 1 pinch of parsley

Directions:

1. Boil the egg, peel it and cut it into large cubes.
2. Put it on the salad plate.
3. Chop the onions into rings and add them.
4. Add the chopped parsley.
5. Then drizzle olive oil over it. Add the 5 drops of lemon. Too much lemon will spoil the taste

of this dish. Add salt and spices and mix
gently.

Smoothie With Leaves, Sprouts And Moringa

Ingredients:

- 60g romaine lettuce leaves

- 15g beetroot leaves

- 5g parsley

- 5g alfalfa sprouts

- 15g radish sprouts

- 1 tablespoon of moringa powder

- 500ml water, for mixing

- 2 dried figs

- 2 dried dates, pitted

- 150ml water for soaking

- 160g apricots

- 1 small banana

- 20g Swiss chard leaves

- 10g celery leaves

Directions:

1. The first thing to do is to soak the figs and dates. Simply put each in 75ml water and 2h. leave.

2. In the meantime, the other Ingredients: can be prepared. Simply cut the apricots in half and stone them.

3. After peeling the banana, cut it into small pieces. Only wash the green leafy vegetables, except for the Swiss chard, where the stalks have to be removed.

4. Now it's time to mix. To do this, put the fruits and leafy vegetables in the blender, add the dates and figs along with the soaking water and the remaining 500ml of water.

5. Put a few of the sprouts aside as a decoration and mix the rest with them.

6. Mix until it has a creamy consistency. Possibly add a little more water.

Quinoa Breakfast Muffins

Ingredients:

- 2 eggs

- 360ml water

- 1 tbsp parsley

- 1 tbsp italian herbs

- 180g quinoa

- 75g baby spinach leaves

- 50g gouda

- Salt

- Pepper

Directions:

1. While the oven is preheating to 180 ° C, let the quinoa soak in a saucepan with hot water over low heat for 15 minutes until the water is completely absorbed.

2. Meanwhile, wash and roughly chop the spinach leaves. The Gouda must be grated or finely cut. Now mix all Ingredients: together and divide evenly on muffin cups.

3. Bake the molds in the oven for 15 minutes. Let cool and serve.

Avocado Mash On Multigrain Toast

Ingredients:

- 1-2 lemons, preferably Meyers, halved

- Aleppo pepper or other crushed red pepper flakes

- Salt, preferably flaky sea salt like Maldon

- 4 slices multigrain bread

- extra virgin olive oil

- 4 ripe Hass avocados, halved, pitted, and peeled

Directions:

1. Toast the bread, then drizzle on one side with the   extra virgin olive oil while still warm.

2. Put 2 avocado halves on each piece of toast and mash them with a butter knife or fork,

spreading the soft fruit to the edges of the
toast.

3. Drizzle the avocados with some   extra virgin
    olive oil. Squeeze some lemon juice over the
    toasts, sprinkle with a pinch or two of Aleppo
    pepper, and season with salt.

4.   Serve with lemon halves.

Saffron Farro With Apricots And Pine Nuts

Ingredients:

- 1.5 ounces Mariani Dried California Apricots, chopped (to size of raisins) (about 1/4 cup chopped)

- 6 cups water

- 1 1/2 teaspoons fine grain sea salt

- 1/2 teaspoon saffron threads

- 2 tablespoons   extra virgin olive oil

- 1/4 cup pine nuts

- 1 medium yellow onion, chopped

- 2 cups Bob's Red Mill Organic Farro, rinsed

Directions:

1. Heat the oil in a medium-size heavy saucepan
    over medium heat. Add the pine nuts and
    cook, stirring constantly, until they are golden
    brown, about 1 to 2 minutes. Immediately
    transfer the pine nuts to a small bowl and set
    aside.

2. Add the onion to the same saucepan and cook
    until softened and just starting to brown,
    about 5 to 7 minutes, stirring occasionally.
    Add the farro and cook for two minutes,
    continuing to stir frequently.

3. Stir in the apricots, water, salt, and saffron,
    then turn the heat up to high, and bring it to a
    rolling boil.

4. Give the farro a stir and then place the lid on
    the saucepan, reduce the heat to medium-low
    and simmer for 30 minutes. (Do not open the
    lid during this time.) Turn the heat off and let
    the farro sit (covered) for 5 minutes and then
    gently fluff with a fork.

5. Drain off any excess liquid and then transfer
    the farro to a serving dish and sprinkle the
    toasted pine nuts on top and serve.

Slow Roasted Romas

Ingredients:

- 4-5 cloves crushed/minced garlic

- 10 basil leaves, cut in chiffonade with scissors

- 10 Roma tomatoes, cut in half the long way, seeds removed

- Small pinch sugar

- 4 Tsp extra virgin olive oil

- Kosher salt & coarse pepper

- Optional: Thyme or Oregano

Directions:

1. Preheat oven to 200, line baking sheet with foil and add 2-3 Tsp extra virgin olive oil to foil.

2. Add garlic, salt and pepper and herbs to oil, then spread around on foil.

3. Cut romas in half lengthwise, scoop out seeds and place face down in oil and herbs.

4. Brush tops of romas with   extra virgin olive oil, sprinkle with a little salt and sugar.

5. Bake for 2 1/2 hours, flipping tomatoes halfway through; open oven briefly every 30 minutes to release excess moisture.

Twice Baked Breakfast Potatoes

Ingredients:

- 3 tablespoons overwhelming cream

- 4 rashers cooked bacon

- 4 huge eggs

- ½ cup destroyed cheddar

- Daintily cut chives

- 2 medium reddish brown potatoes, cleaned and pricked with a fork everywhere

- 2 tablespoons unsalted spread

- Salt and pepper to taste

Directions:

1. Preheat grill to 400°F.

2. Spot potatoes straightforwardly on stove rack In the focus of the grill and steel oneself against 30 to 45 min.

3. Evacuate and permit potatoes to chill for around a quarter-hour.

4. Cut every potato down the center longwise and burrow every half out, scooping the potato substance into a blending bowl.

5. Gather margarine and cream to the potato and pound into one unit until smooth — season with salt and pepper and blend.

6. Spread some of the potato blends into the bottom of every emptied potato peel and sprinkle with one tablespoon cheddar (you may make them remain pounded potato left to snack on).

7. Add one rasher bacon to each half and top with a raw egg.

8. Spot potatoes onto a heating sheet and are available back to the appliance.

9. Lower broiler temperature to 375°F and warm potatoes until egg whites simply set and yolks are so far runny.

10. Top every potato with a sprinkle of the remainder of the cheddar, season with salt and pepper, and finish with cut chives.

Blueberry Muffins

Ingredients:

- ½ cup unsweetened almond milk

- 2–3 tablespoons maple syrup

- 2 tablespoons coconut oil, melted

- 1 cup fresh blueberries

- 1 cup buckwheat flour

- 1½ teaspoons baking powder

- ¼ teaspoon of sea salt

- 2 eggs

Directions:

1. Preheat your oven to 350ºF and line 8 cups of a muffin tin.

2. In a bowl, place the buckwheat flour, leaven, and salt, and blend well.

3. In a separate bowl, place the eggs, almond milk, syrup, and copra oil, and beat until well combined.

4. Now, place the flour mixture and blend until just combined.

5. Gently fold In the blueberries.

6. Transfer the mixture into prepared muffin cups evenly.

7. Bake for about 25 minutes or until a toothpick inserted In the center comes out clean.

8. Remove the muffin tin from the oven and place onto a wire rack to chill for about 10 minutes.

9. Carefully invert the muffins onto the wire rack to chill completely before serving.

Quick Sirtfood Chicken Salad

Ingredients:

- Chopped coriander, 1 tsp

- Curry powder, ½ tsp

- Chopped walnuts, 1 cup

- 2 finely chopped Medjool dates

- Arugula, 1 cup

- 1 bird's eye chili

- Diced chicken breasts, 5 oz

- Greek yogurt, 1 cup

- Lime juice, 1 tbsp

- Ground turmeric, 1 tsp

- 1 diced red onion

Directions:

1. Cook chicken breasts until ready per your taste and set aside to cool down.

2. Mix the dry Ingredients: into a bowl, add the chicken breasts, top with lime juice and extra virgin olive oil.

Braised Leek With Pine Nuts

Ingredients:

- 1 tablespoon new oregano

- tablespoon Pine nuts (simmered)

- 2 teaspoon Olive oil 2 pieces Leek

- 20 g Ghee

- 150 ml Vegetable stock new parsley

Directions:

1. Cut the leek into thin rings and finely slice the herbs. Cook the pine nuts in a dry pan over medium warmth.

2. Melt the ghee along with the olive oil in a huge pan.

3. Cook the leek until brilliant brown for 5 minutes, blending continually.

4. Include the vegetable stock and cook for an additional 10 minutes until the leek is delicate.

5. Mix in the herbs and sprinkle the pine nuts on the dish not long before serving.

Fruit And Crunchy Nut Yogurt

Ingredients:

- 50 grams (2 ounces) strawberries, chopped

- 6 walnut halves, chopped

- A Sprinkling of cocoa powder

- 100 grams (3(½) ounces) plain Greek yogurt

Directions:

1. Stir half of the chopped strawberries into the yogurt.

2. Using a glass, place a layer of yogurt with a sprinkling of strawberries and walnuts, followed by another layer of the same until you reach the top of the glass.

3. Garnish with walnuts pieces and a dusting of cocoa powder.

anana And Cinnamon Oatmeal

Ingredients:

- 1 teaspoon ground cinnamon

- 2 chopped large ripe bananas

- 4 teaspoons brown sugar

- 2 cups quick-cooking oats

- 4 cups fat-free milk

- Extra ground cinnamon

Directions:

1. Place milk in a skillet and bring to boil. Add oats and cook over medium heat until thickened for two to four minutes.

2. Stir intermittently.

3. Add cinnamon, brown sugar and banana, and stir to combine.

4. If you want, serve with the extra cinnamon

and milk. Enjoy!

Summer Berry Smoothie

Ingredients:

- 25g (1 ounces) blackcurrants

- 25g (1 ounces) red grapes

- 1 carrot, peeled

- 1 orange, peeled

- 50g (2 ounces) blueberries

- 50g (2 ounces) strawberries

- Juice of 1 lime

Directions:

1. Place all of the Ingredients: into a blender and cover them with water.

2. Blitz until smooth. You can also add some crushed ice and a mint leaf to garnish.

Mango, Celery & Ginger Smoothie

Ingredients:

- 1 apple, cored

- 50g (2 ounces) mango, peeled, de-stoned and chopped

- 2.5cm (1 inch) chunk of fresh ginger root, peeled and chopped

- 1 stalk of celery

- 50g (2ounces) kale

Directions:

1. Put all the Ingredients: into a blender with some water and blitz until smooth. Add ice to make your smoothie really refreshing.

Mushroom Buckwheat Pancakes

Ingredients:

- 1.94 ounce wholemeal flour

- 1.94 ounce buckwheat flour

- 9 ounce Alpro Almond Milk

- 2 free-range egg

- 1.05 ounce butter, for frying

For the filling:

- 4 large handfuls of baby spinach

- Olive oil

- 9 ounce Alpro Almond Milk

- 2 free-range egg

- 1.76 ounce flour

- 1.76 ounce butter

- 9 ounce Alpro Almond Milk

- 2 free-range egg3.52 ounce sliced chestnut mushrooms

Directions:

1. Melt butter in a saucepan 1.76 ounce. Use the flour to create a paste. Continue cooking for 30 seconds.

2. Gradually add the milk, stirring vigorously until the white sauce is smooth. (Make sure to stir well so that lumps do not form.)

3. Fry the mushrooms in the oil until the spinach is brown and wilt. Drop the mushrooms into the white sauce, add the cheese and nutmeg to taste, then season.

4. In the meantime, add the two flour types to a bowl, and make a small well.

5. Whisk the egg into the milk, lightly. Pour a handful of the egg mixture into the flour and continue whisking.

6. Start applying the liquid and whisking until the batter is smooth.

7. Melt the butter and add a ladle of the batter in a non-stick frying pan. Swirl to brush the

base of the pan equally, then turn it as the
pancake is shakeable.

8. Repeat until all the batter has been
    consumed, and then line it with mushroom
    and spinach stuffing.

Tuscan Bean Stew

Ingredients:

- 1/2 thai, finely chopped chili (optional)

- 1 herbs de provence teaspoon

- Vegetable stock: 7/8 cup (200ml)

- 1 x 14-unce (400 g) of italian chopped tomatoes

- 1 pureed tomato tablespoon

- Drained weight: 3/4 cup (130 g) canned mixed beans

- Cup 3/4 (50 g) kale, about chopped

- 1 tablespoon of approximately chopped parsley

- 1 litre, extra virgin olive oil

- 1/3 cup (50 g) red, finely chopped onion

- 1/4 cup (30 g) carrot, finely chopped and peeled

- 1/3 cup (30 g) celery, finely chopped and trimmed

- 2 cloves of garlic, finely chopped

- Buckwheat: 1/4 cup (40 g)

Directions:

1. Place the oil over low to medium heat in a medium saucepan and fry the onion, carrot, celery, garlic, chili (if used) and herbs gently, until the onion is soft but not browned.

2. Stir in the collection, tomatoes and purée tomatoes and bring to a boil. Attach the beans and require to cook for 30 minutes.

3. Add the kale and simmer for another 5 to 10 minutes, then add the parsley, until tender.

4. Meanwhile, according to the box instructions, cook the buckwheat, rinse and then serve with the stew.

Strawberry Tabbouleh Bukkwheat

Ingredients:

- 1 tablelit capers

- Petersil: 3/4 cup (30 g)

- 2/3 cup (100 g) hulled strawberries

- 1 litre, extra virgin olive oil

- 1/2 lemon juice

- Buckwheat: 1/3 cup (50 g)

- 1 tablespoon of turmeric soil

- 1/2 cup avocado (80 g)

- Tomatoes: 3/8 cup (65 g)

- 1/8 cup red onion (20 g)

- 1/8 cup (25 g) dates medjool, pitted

- 1 ounce arugula (30 g)

Directions:

1. Cook the buckwheat with the turmeric as indicated on the box. Drain to cool, and set aside.

2. Chop the avocado, basil, red onion, dates, capers and parsley thinly and mix with the fresh buckwheat. Pick the strawberries, then mix the oil then lemon juice softly into the salad. Serve on an earthenware bed.

Baked Cod Miso-Marinated With Stir-Fried Greens And Sesame

Ingredients:

- 1 thai chili, finely chopped

- 1 teaspoon of fresh ginger, finely chopped

- 3/8 cup green beans (60 g)

- Cup 3/4 (50 g) kale, about chopped

- 1 sesame seeds in tablespoon

- 2 tablespoons (5 g) of parsley, chopped roughly

- 1 tablespoon tamari (or soy sauce, unless gluten is avoided)

- Buckwheat: 1/4 cup (40 g)

- 31/2 cups of tea (20 g) miso

- 1 tablelitre mirin

- 1 litre, extra virgin olive oil

- 1 x 7-ounce (200 g) filet of skinless cod

- 1/8 cup (20 g) raw, sliced onion

- Celery: 3/8 cup (40 g), sliced

- 2 cloves of garlic, finely chopped

- 1 teaspoon of turmeric powder

Directions:

1. Mix the oil with the miso, mirin and 1 tablespoon. Rub the cod all over, and set for 30 minutes to marinate. Heat the oven to 220 ° C (425oF).

2. Bake the cod for about 10 minutes.

3. Meanwhile, heat the remaining oil to a large frying pan or wok. Stir-fry the onion for a few minutes, then add the celery, garlic, chili, ginger, green beans and kale.

4. Toss and fry until the kale is cooked through and tender. To help the cooking process you might need to add a little water to the pan.

5. Cook the buckwheat along with the turmeric according to the packet instructions.

6. To the stir-fry add the sesame seeds, parsley, and tamari and serve with buckwheat and shrimp.

Salad With Arugula

Ingredients:

- 2 cloves of garlic

- 1 pinch of parsley

- 1 lemon

- 4 walnuts

- 1 bunch of arugula

- 1 small red onion

- 2 sprigs of scallions

Directions:

1. Chop the arugula. Chop the red onions into rings. Put them in a salad bowl. Then add the crushed garlic and finely chopped parsley.

2. Squeeze the juice of the lemon, add it to the
    salad and mix well. Garnish with 4 finely
    chopped walnuts.

Smoked Salmon Omelette

Ingredients:

- 1 tsp parsley – chopped

- 1 tbsp olive oil

- 2 large organic eggs

- 5 slices of smoked salmon

- 1 tbsp capers

- 2 cups arugula – chopped

Directions:

1. Crack your eggs in a small bowl and whisk them well.

2. Continue by adding your sliced salmon, capers, arugula and parsley and stir gently.

3. In a nonstick pan, add your olive oil and heat until hot but not smoking.

4. Add your egg mixture and using a spatula
    spread the mixture until all the pan is covered
    and even. Lower your heat and allow the
    omelet to cook through.

5. Once cooked through use the spatula to fold
    the omelet in half and serve it along with our
    favorite cup of coffee.

Matcha With Vanilla

Ingredients:

- ½ tspmatcha powder

- seeds from half a vanilla pod

Directions:

1. Boil the kettle then pour 100ml of the water into a measuring jug. Pour half the hot water into a small bowl, to warm it, then add the matcha powder and vanilla seeds to the rest of the water in the jug.

2. Whisk the mixture with a bamboo match whisk or mini electric whisk until it's smooth, lump-free and slightly bubbly. Discard the water in the warmed tea bowl, then pour in the prepared matcha tea.

Green Breakfast Omlette

Ingredients:

- 0.5 avocado

- 50ml milk

- 10g basil

- salt

- pepper

- 3 eggs

- 200g canned peas

- 200g of grainy cream cheese

- Oil for frying

Directions:

1. First, the milk and basil are pureed into a
   frothy mass with the help of a hand blender.
2. Now add half of the peas to the milk
   mixture. Add the beaten eggs, season to taste
   and puree everything again.
3. Fry the mass in a pan with oil.
4. Cover the finished omelette with cream
   cheese, avocado slices and the remaining peas
   and serve.